IT WORKS!
Revolution in
Medicine

Lynette Brent Sandvold

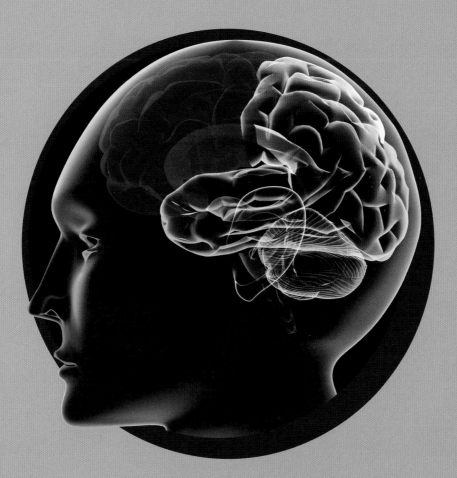

 **Marshall Cavendish**
Benchmark
New York

This edition first published in 2010 in the United States
of America by Marshall Cavendish Benchmark.

Marshall Cavendish Benchmark
99 White Plains Road
Tarrytown, NY 10591
www.marshallcavendish.us

Library of Congress Cataloging-in-Publication Data

Sandvold, Lynette Brent.
Revolution in medicine / by Lynette Brent Sandvold.
p. cm. -- (It works!)
Summary: "Discusses the history of medicine, how the technology developed,
and the science behind it"--Provided by publisher.
Includes bibliographical references and index.
ISBN 978-0-7614-4376-6
1. Medicine--History--Juvenile literature.
2. Medical technology--Juvenile literature. I. Title.
R133.5.S26 2010
610.9--dc22
2008054364

Cover: Q2AMedia Art Bank
Half Title: Shutterstock.
P7tl: Reefer/Dreamstime; P7bl: Scott Olson/Getty Images; P7tr: Reises/Fotolia;
P7cr: Godrick/Dreamstime; P7br: Hulton Archive/Getty Images; P11: Bettmann/
CORBIS; P11tr: Dennis D Bayley/iStockphoto; P11br: LWA-Dann Tardif/Corbis;
P15: Bettmann/Corbis; P15bl: Liza McCorkle/iStockphoto; P15br: Wayne Conradie/
Corbis; P19tr: JP Laffont/Sygma/Corbis; P19br: Nilgun Bostanci/iStockphoto;
P23: Daniel Quat/Photolibrary; P27(inset)bl: Jupiter Images; P27(inset)tm: Scott Hirko/
iStockphoto; P27(inset)bm: Bob Grahame; P27R: Oxford Scientifc/Photolibrary.
Illustrations: Q2AMedia Art Bank

Created by Q2AMedia
Series Editor: Jessica Cohn
Art Director: Sumit Charles
Client Service Manager: Santosh Vasudevan
Project Manager: Shekhar Kapur
Designer: Shilpi Sarkar
Illustrators: Aadil Ahmed, Indranil Ganguly,
Rishi Bhardwaj, Kusum Kala and Sanyogita Lal
Photo research: Shreya Sharma

Printed in Malaysia

1 3 5 6 4 2

Contents

Fighting a Headache

Have you heard of **acetylsalicylic acid**? That may sound like something from a mad scientist's laboratory. Acetylsalicylic acid is aspirin!

Long ago, doctors realized that bark from a willow tree could kill pain. In the 19th century, scientists discovered the pain-killing ingredient in willow bark. They called it salicylic acid. Taken on its own, that acid caused stomach pain. Finding it didn't do much good. Then chemist Felix Hoffman mixed it with another acid. That mixture made a new medicine. It made aspirin. The new medicine was easier to stomach. It was easy to make. It was also inexpensive.

Over 70 million pounds of aspirin are produced around the world each year. People use aspirin for headaches and muscle aches. Aspirin can help prevent heart attacks. It can also treat strokes and even help with certain cancers.

Meet Felix Hoffman

Felix Hoffman was born in Germany in 1868. He studied chemistry and became a **pharmacist.** Hoffman worked at Bayer Company when he developed aspirin. He wasn't looking to be famous or make money. His main reason for creating aspirin was to help his father. His father suffered from painful **arthritis**. Hoffman made his discovery almost by accident. He combined a few different acids. He found a drug for pain that he could make at a low cost. Bayer became famous for being the first company to sell aspirin. Hoffman was never famous himself, though.

Sixty-five years ago, Charles Gergardt mixed salicylic acid with another chemical, making a new medicine. The medicine took a long time to make, however.

His invention wasn't practical, so he put it aside. I think there must be a better way.

People don't believe aspirin will work. My boss called the idea "worthless."

Their minds will change when they see how much my new mix has helped my dad!

Fastest Relief for Pain

spoons, if you
stir the samples

different pain relievers,
such as aspirin, ibuprofen,
and coated aspirin

water

household acid,
such as lemon
juice or vinegar

clear drinking glasses,
one for each kind of
pain reliever

clock or
stopwatch

helpers, if you have many
pain relievers to test

1 Pour the lemon juice or vinegar in equal amounts in the glasses. Add a bit of water, in equal amounts. The acid will work as your stomach acid does.

2 In each glass, place one pain reliever. Observe what happens.

3 You can stir the samples, but be sure that you treat each sample the same. For example, friends need to help so all are stirred equally and at the same time.

4 Use the clock or stopwatch to figure out which dissolves fastest. Which pain reliever would enter your bloodstream fastest?

WHO WOULD HAVE THOUGHT?

Hippocrates and Modern Medicine

Hippocrates lived thousands of years ago. He is called the Father of Modern Medicine. During his lifetime, many doctors believed that evil spirits caused illnesses. Hippocrates observed the human body. He linked illness to physical causes. He was one of the first to tell patients that exercise, fresh air, cleanliness, and rest would help. He was the first doctor who realized that thoughts come from the brain rather than the heart. Hippocrates made a powder from the bark and leaves of the willow tree. It helped people get rid of aches and pains. The main ingredient in his powder was the same used in today's aspirin!

garlic chives,
for pneumonia

cardoon leaves,
for wounds

Hippocrates,
Father of Modern
Medicine

willow tree,
for pain

Call for First Aid

Did you ever cut your finger on something sharp? Did you wash the cut and put a Band-Aid™ on it? That can protect a cut while it heals. Less than one hundred years ago, though, there was no such thing.

Earle Dickson invented this everyday item in 1921. His wife was always cutting her fingers when cooking! Back then, people cut **adhesive tape** and **gauze** to the right size to cover wounds. It took a while to get out the supplies. It took more time to cut them to size and put them on. Then there was another problem. The tape could quickly lose its stick. Dickson's wife was active. Her fingers were always moving! He wanted to create something quick and with staying power.

Meet Earle Dickson

Earle Dickson wasn't a doctor. He was a cotton buyer for a company called Johnson and Johnson. He wasn't trying to become a famous inventor when he invented ready-made bandages. He was trying to help his wife! Dickson's boss liked the idea, though. He put the bandages into production. Sales were slow until the company gave away Band-Aids™ to Boy Scout troops. Then the product caught on. Three years later, the company put in machines to make them. The product was so successful that Dickson was made vice president of the company.

Using gauze and tape takes too long. Bandages need to be smaller and have more "stick." Otherwise, they fall off.

I put the gauze pad right on the tape. I covered the tape with cloth to help keep the gauze even cleaner.

The smaller size helps the bandage stay in place.

These bandages don't cure cuts, but they can keep **infections** from developing.

9

Test Bandages for "Stick"

4 types of bandages

4 weights that will sink in water

stopwatch or clock

Paper and pencil for averaging & labeling

small bucket filled with water

1 Label the weights and bandages with numbers 1 through 4, one number for each. You'll need this for recordkeeping.

2 Place a bandage on each of the weights. Record the time. Then carefully lower the weights into the water.

3 Start timing. Record the time that the bandage comes off each of the weights.

4 Repeat until you can figure out the average time for the adhesive to stick. What do your results tell you about how often you should change a bandage?

WHO WOULD HAVE THOUGHT?

Getting and Staying Well

In the mid-1800s, many patients died from infections following surgeries. Doctors believed that air was causing the infections. So they tightly covered wounds with plasters, mixtures of sand, lime, and water. One surgeon, Joseph Lister, thought there had to be another reason for the infections. He had heard that you could put carbolic acid on fields to cure sick cattle. So Lister created a mix with carbolic acid. He used it to wash wounds. Patients treated this way were more likely to live. Other surgeons began to use steam to **sterilize** surgical instruments. They realized that Lister was right. It wasn't the air that hurt; it was germs!

Doctors used to use steam to keep things clean.

Calling the Shots

S hots, also called injections or vaccinations, help keep us healthy. Needles deliver fluids into our bodies. For example, if we lose blood after an accident, needles help give us new blood. Doctors and nurses also use needles to draw blood for tests.

It wasn't until 1853 that Charles Gabriel Pravaz and Alexander Wood invented a **syringe**. The new tool had a needle narrow enough to pierce skin. Its first use was to inject morphine. That is a powerful painkiller. The first mass-produced throwaway syringes were made in the 1950s. They were used for the **polio** vaccine. Years later, other inventors made syringes of plastic instead of glass.

Today, microneedles deliver medicine. A microneedle is a patch with hundreds of tiny needles, each as thin as a human hair. The thin needles do not touch nerves. The patient does not feel pain!

I WAS FIRST!

I WAS!

Meet Charles Gabriel Pravaz and Alexander Wood

Alexander Wood and Charles Gabriel Pravaz worked independently on the **hypodermic** syringe. They are both given credit for the invention. Wood was born in Scotland in 1817. Pravaz, a French physician, was born in 1791. Before their invention, doctors used needles to put medicine into people's bodies. The needles, however, could not pierce the skin. Doctors had to use natural body openings. Sometimes they cut open the skin to get the needles inside people. The new, thinner needles allowed for quick pain relief. They also made for quick delivery of pain-killing drugs for surgery. Before people knew to clean them right, however, needles also spread disease.

A hollow needle allows for quick delivery of a drug.

Needles need to be narrow and sharp to pass through the skin.

Passing the needle directly into the skin saves the step of cutting through the skin. It also saves time in an emergency.

Syringes use the science of air pressure and vacuums to push materials into the body and to take them out.

Watch Air Pressure Work

funnel

two- or three-liter
plastic soda bottle

duct tape

pitcher

1 Place the funnel in the bottle. Use duct tape to tape the funnel into the bottle with an airtight seal.

2 Fill the pitcher with water. Set the bottle and funnel in the sink. Quickly fill the bottle with water so that the water level rises in the funnel. Keep pouring until the water is near the top of the funnel.

3 Place your hand tightly over the top of the funnel. Turn the bottle upside down, keeping your hand on the bottom of the funnel.

4 The water doesn't fall into the funnel because of air pressure. The pressure on the outside of the bottle keeps the water from coming out.

WHO WOULD HAVE THOUGHT?

Vaccinations and a Cure

In the 1950s, one in every five thousand children who had polio died. Children who survived were often unable to walk. Scientists raced to figure out a way to stop the disease. Jonas Salk used the work of many scientists to come up with a vaccination. He produced large amounts of the polio virus. He then killed the virus and used the killed virus to make a vaccine. He injected his wife, his sons, and himself with it. Everyone who received the vaccine produced **antibodies.** No one got sick! Soon, children began receiving vaccinations. A few years later, a "live" vaccine was introduced. Children could eat that vaccine on a sugar cube rather than getting a shot. A little over half a century later, there are few cases of polio in the world.

Dr. Jonas Salk

Listening to the Heart

Rene Laennec was a thirty-five-year-old doctor in France. While walking to work in 1816, he noticed two children sending signals to each other. They were using a long piece of wood and a pin. One child scratched one end of the wood with a pin. The other child put her ear to the other end of the wood. She could hear the scratching.

Laennec thought about what he had seen. Could he figure out a way to bring heart sounds closer to his ear? That would save his patients the embarrassment they felt when he pressed his ear to their chests. He invented the **stethoscope** to explore the chest. The word *stethoscope* comes from the Greek words *stethos* (chest) and *skopein* (explore).

Meet Rene Laennec

Rene Theophile Hyacinthe Laennec was born in France in 1781. His mother died when he was young. His family sent him to live with his uncle, a medical school professor. Laennec was bright. He earned prizes for work in medicine and surgery before he was twenty years old. He was one of the first doctors to identify **pneumonia**. He didn't just use his stethoscope to listen to heartbeats. He also discovered many things about the chest. He wrote a groundbreaking book about using the stethoscope. Most of his ideas and ways of doing things are still used today.

Place your ear to one end of a piece of wood. You can hear a slight scratch made on the other end.

I use a roll of paper and put one end near my ear and the other near my patient's chest. I can hear the heart beating more clearly than with just my ear.

With a hollow wooden tube, I can listen more closely to a patient's heart beating.

I could use my new instrument to listen to all the sounds in the chest, including in the lungs.

How Sound Travels Best

3 self-sealing bags   sand   water   pencil   partner

1 Fill one self-sealing bag with sand. Seal it tightly, making sure there is no air left in the bag.

2 Fill another bag with water, again making sure there is no air in the bag. Seal it tightly.

3 Fill the final bag with air. Seal it tightly. Put all the bags on a table.

4 Put one ear to a bag. Cover the other ear with a hand. Listen as your partner taps the table with a pencil. Does sound travel better through sand, air, or water?

WHO WOULD HAVE THOUGHT?

Broken Hearts

Your heart is an amazing muscle. It pumps blood and oxygen throughout your body. That is why many people with heart failure need heart transplants. Many of them die because so few hearts are available. Artificial hearts, though, can help some of those patients stay alive until a heart is ready. In 1982, Barney Clark was the first person given an artificial heart, the **Jarvik-7**. Clark lived 112 days after the surgery. There is now a newer artificial heart, the AbioCor. It uses hydraulic systems to pump blood through the body. The patients who have received the artificial heart have lived an average of five months afterward. The heart is so complex it's hard for a machine to take its place forever.

Jarvik–7

artery

vein

Laser Vision

The shape of the eye can cause sight problems. If you have trouble seeing distant objects, your eyeball may be too long. If you cannot see objects close up, your eyeball may be too short. People with sight problems can usually correct them. Eyeglasses and contact lenses are both things that people use to see better.

In **laser** surgery, a surgeon can use a laser to reshape parts of the eye. First, the surgeon cuts a flap on the outer part of the eye. Then a laser reshapes the tissue underneath. The flap is then replaced. The eye begins to heal almost immediately. The surgery is possible because of a special tool, the excimer laser. Dr. Stephen Trokel was a pioneer in this kind of laser surgery. Now, lasers do many things. They smooth out wrinkles. They unclog arteries. Arteries are the blood vessels that carry blood away from the heart.

Meet Stephen Trokel

Long ago, comic books showed superheroes with laser vision. Now many real people have had their sight helped by lasers! Dr. Stephen Trokel was the first doctor to perform laser surgery on a patient's eyes. His first laser eye surgery was in 1987. He spent a decade improving both the equipment and the way to use it. In the 1970s the excimer laser was used to cut into computer chips. Dr. Trokel, however, gets credit for using this laser for sight correction. The excimer laser was approved for eye surgeries in the United States in 1996.

I saw what an excimer laser could do with computer chips. The laser did not heat up surfaces around itself.

So I made a laser for eye surgery. It does not cause heat damage to the rest of the eye.

The laser can quickly reshape the eye.

The eye heals very fast. The results are almost instantaneous!

21

Make a Model of the Eye

round, clear glass bowl with water inside

sheet of cardboard covered with black paper

cardboard covered with white paper

small table lamp without a shade

pencil

1 Use the pencil to poke a small hole in the middle of the black cardboard. Stand the black cardboard against one side of the bowl. Stand the white cardboard on the other side, opposite the black cardboard.

2 Turn on the lamp. Place it so that it is shining through the hole in the black cardboard. Darken the room as much as possible.

3 The hole acts like the eye's pupil. Move the white board from side to side until an image of the lamp shows up.

4 The water bowl acts like the eyeball. Its curve makes an image appear upside down. The brain makes an image from the eyes appear right side up.

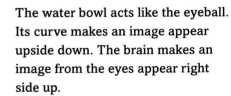 

WHO WOULD HAVE THOUGHT?

Doctors, Dentists, and Lasers

In 1960, Theodore Maiman, a scientist and an engineer, created the first working *laser,* short for Light Amplification by Stimulated Emission of Radiation. (*Radiation* is a way to talk about traveling light.) Scientists can use tubes to channel very narrow beams of light. The tubes pass the light beams through a crystal or gas. These strong, narrow beams have all kinds of uses in medicine. Researchers are even using lasers for finding disease and removing **cancerous** tissue. They are also researching ways to heal broken bones and help burned skin grow back. The excimer laser used in eye surgeries can focus a beam that is 25 microns. That's small! A human hair is about 50 microns in diameter.

Lasers are used in industry, too.

Get an Inside Look

Doctors use Xrays to see broken bones. Airport security uses Xrays to peek inside our bags. Xrays in factories weld metals. Archaeologists can use Xrays to see what's under a mummy's wrappings! Who discovered these rays? It was a scientist named Wilhelm Roentgen.

What are Xrays? They are waves of **electromagnetic energy**, much like light you can see. Xrays travel in streams of tiny light **particles**. These streams can pass into the human body. Different body parts take in the particles, called photons, in different ways. Soft body tissue cannot absorb and hold photons well. So soft body tissue does not show up on an Xray. Your bones have calcium. Calcium does absorb Xray photons. When an Xray camera aims at your body, the bones can be seen. The bones are recorded on special camera film.

Meet Wilhelm Roentgen

Wilhelm Roentgen, born in 1845, was a German physicist. He discovered Xrays almost by accident. In 1895, he was experimenting with electron beams and tubes. He noticed that a screen in his lab was glowing. He was surprised because he had surrounded the tube with heavy black cardboard. The cardboard should have blocked the radiation. He then started experimenting. He held up different objects between the tube and the screen. The scientist put his hand in front of the tube. He saw the outline of his bones projected onto the screen.

I discovered a new kind of radiation. Because I'm not sure what it's made of, I am calling it X-radiation.

X-radiation can pass through many materials, like parts of the body that usually take in regular light.

When I pass the new light through most body parts, the rays go through without showing anything. I can see bones and most metals, though.

Bending Bones

chicken bone (a leg bone works best)

jar large enough to fit the bone

vinegar

 1 Rinse the chicken bone in water to remove the meat. Try gently bending the bone. You'll notice that the bone is hard. The strength in bone comes from calcium.

2 Put the bone in the jar. Pour enough vinegar in the jar to cover the bone. Put a lid on the jar and let it sit for three days.

 3 Remove the bone. Rinse it off and try bending it again. The acid in the vinegar is strong enough to eat away at the calcium in bone. Now you know why calcium is so important!

 4 Try the experiment with other animal parts from your home, such as lobster claws, seashells, and eggshells. What can you conclude about the amount of calcium in each?

WHO WOULD HAVE THOUGHT?

Magnetic Resonance Imaging

An MRI (magnetic resonance imaging) is a newer kind of medical test than an Xray. Doctors performed the first one in 1977. An MRI gives amazing pictures. They help doctors do things like pinpoint where healthy tissue in the body ends and cancerous tissue begins. An MRI uses magnetic fields rather than light to make images. How? **Hydrogen nuclei** in the human body line up with a strong magnetic field in the MRI machine. Then a different magnetic field pushes those nuclei out of line. The nuclei of different kinds of tissues move at different speeds. So the images show differences in the tissues in action. Doctors can pinpoint places that are not right. New things are happening in medicine all the time!

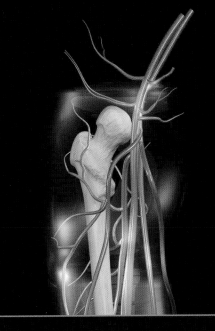

MRI machine

Airport Xray shows contents of a suitcase.

MRI image of a knee joint

portable Xray

Timeline

420 B.C.
Hippocrates says that diseases have natural causes.

1816
Rene Laennec invents the stethoscope.

1853
Charles Gabriel Pravaz and Alexander Wood invent a syringe needle narrow enough to pierce skin.

1867
Joseph Lister publishes *Antiseptic Principle of the Practice of Surgery*, based partly on the work of Louis Pasteur.

1895
Wilhelm Conrad Roentgen discovers a medical use for Xrays.

1987
The first laser surgery on a human eye is performed by Dr. Steven Trokel, after he spent nine years practicing on cows' eyes.

1982
Barney Clark becomes the first person to receive an artificial heart.

1962
The first oral polio vaccine is used.

1952
Jonas Salk develops the first polio vaccine.

1921
Earle Dickson makes Band-Aids™.

1897
Felix Hoffman makes aspirin.

Glossary

acetylsalicylic acid aspirin; a substance used to relieve pain.

adhesive tape cotton or other fabric coated with a sticky substance, used for covering skin injuries, holding bandages in place, and so on.

antibody substance produced by the body to fight disease-causing germs.

arthritis inflammation of a joint, a place where two bones meet.

cancerous having cancer, a disease in which cells grow out of bounds.

electromagnetic energy the power within and outside a magnetic field produced by movements of electrons; electrons are the particles that move around the nucleus of an atom and have a negative electrical charge.

gauze very thin cloth that you can see through; gauze is used in making bandages.

hydrogen nuclei the centers, or nuclei, of hydrogen atoms.

hypodermic under the skin, as in a hollow needle used to inject things under the skin.

infection disease caused by germs entering the body.

Jarvik-7 special artificial heart for the human body.

laser device that produces a strong, narrow beam of light by exciting atoms and causing them to send out their energy a certain way.

particle tiny bit of something.

pharmacist person qualified to prepare and give out drugs.

pneumonia disease in which the lungs become inflamed and fill with thick fluid; pneumonia is caused by a virus.

polio disease that can cause paralysis by attacking the spinal cord. It is caused by a virus.

sterilize to free from dirt or germs.

stethoscope instrument used to carry sounds in the chest or other parts of the body to the ear of someone listening.

syringe small device made of a glass, metal, or hard rubber tube, narrowed at its outlet, and fitted with either a piston or a rubber bulb for drawing in or sending out fluid.

To Learn More

Books

Health and Medicine (Science News for Kids) by Tara Koellhoffer. Chelsea Clubhouse, 2006.

Medical Marvels by Catherine Nichols. Scholastic Library, 2004.

National Geographic Investigates: Medical Mysteries: Science Researches Conditions from Bizarre to Deadly by Scott Auden. National Geographic Children's Books, 2008.

Websites

Enchanted Learning lists interesting inventors and inventions related to medicine and hygiene . . . from A to Z!
http://www.enchantedlearning.com/inventors/medicine.shtml

The Merck Institute for Science Education details a decade's worth of the most promising medical advances. Read about important breakthroughs, from Magnetic Resonance Imaging (MRI) technology to blood substitutes.
http://www.mise.org/mise/index.jsp?p=decade_home

An interactive timeline, from the Association for School Science, reveals important innovations in medicine from prehistoric times to the present.
http://resources.schoolscience.co.uk/abpi/history/index.html

Index